# Bottling Fruit and Vegetables

A Selection of Recipes and Articles

by Various Authors

# Contents

Bottling Soft Fruit *page 1*

Bottling Stone Fruit *page 5*

Bottling Various Fruits and Vegetables *page 10*

Fruit Bottling *page 15*

Home-bottled Fruits and How to do them *page 33*

Bottling or Canning *page 73*

## BOTTLING SOFT FRUIT

THE best soft fruits for bottling are gooseberries, cherries, currants, raspberries, apricots, plums, damsons, blackberries, tomatoes, apples, and pears. Strawberries can also be successfully bottled, but they require more care and trouble than other fruits, because they are so much softer.

*Gooseberries.*—Gooseberries are the easiest of all fruits to bottle, and as a rule give the most satisfactory results. The following directions should be carefully followed. Have the bottles ready, making quite sure that they are perfectly clean and quite dry. The gooseberries should be picked when green and hard, and before they get too large. For bottling they ought always to be picked in the same condition as that in which they are used for green gooseberry tart. Before putting the fruit into the bottles it should be topped and tailed, and to insure a good appearance when finished it is always best to grade the fruit, and only put berries in which are the same size, rejecting any that are too large or not sound, or are disfigured in any way. These can always be used up in the preserving pan. Pack the fruit closely into the jars without bruising, to within an inch of the top, and fill up with cold water or syrup to the very top of the bottle. Do not put on the cap at once, as the water often sinks when it has worked its way down amongst the fruit. If this happens the bottles should be filled up again, as the fruit ought always to be well covered.

*Capping the Bottles.*—The bottles are now ready for

# BOTTLING SOFT FRUIT

capping, and much of the success depends upon the care taken in capping. The indiarubber rings are next put on. Have ready a basin of hot water, and before laying the ring on the mouth of the bottle dip it into the hot water, for a second or two. This makes the rubber more flexible and more likely to lie quite flat, which is an important point. When the ring is in its place put on the metal cap. Care must be taken to place it on the bottle perfectly straight. The spring clip is then put on, and the bottle is ready to go into the steriliser. Imperfect capping is often due to the ring, or the cap being carelessly put on. This allows the air to get in, and prevents the bottle becoming hermetically sealed, as it should be.

*Sterilising the Fruit.*—The bottles are now placed in the steriliser. They should stand just clear of each other. A sufficient quantity of cold water is put in to cover the bottle three parts of the way up. The lid is then put on, and the thermometer screwed into its socket. The temperature generally registered at this stage is about 60°. It is very gradually allowed to rise till it reaches 155°. An increase of two degrees a minute is rapid enough. If the temperature is allowed to go up with a rush the skin of the fruit in the bottles will be cracked. It nearly always takes an hour, if not more, before the required temperature is reached. The bottles should be kept at 155° for 45 minutes. If gas or oil is used for the heating this is easily done by regulating the flame. In the jacketed sterilisers (Mercia) the hot air cushion keeps the temperature very even. At the end of 45 minutes the bottles are taken out and put to cool. If a screw-topped bottle is used, such as the De Lucca or Atlas Fruit Jar, the loose rim is now tightly screwed down. Where the spring clip is used it is left on till the bottles are quite cold. When this stage has been reached (probably the next day) each bottle should be examined to see if the cap is perfectly tight, if so it has become hermetically sealed, and will only move by pressure from without, such as the insertion of a knife between cap and rubber ring to raise it. This will be a proof of the fruit keeping. If any are found imperfectly capped they should be re-sterilised; but a careful examination should be made of the cap, to see if it fits properly or not, as a certain percentage of those sent out are sure to be faulty.

*Cherries.*—The Kentish cherry is excellent for preserving in this way. Pick the cherries off their stalks, and pack in the bottles. The fruit should be firm but nearly ripe. When packing shake the bottle gently up and down, so that the fruit may fit in closely. If the fruit is pricked at one end with a needle it prevents bursting. Fill up the bottles with syrup or water. Proceed as indicated in the foregoing recipe, and sterilise at 150°. Another method is to split the cherries in half with a sharp knife, take out the stones, crack some, and return the kernels to the bottles when packing. This latter method keeps the fruit a beautiful colour, but it would be well to use syrup instead of water, because preserved in this way they are richer in flavour and appearance and sell for a higher price. Unless in a cherry-growing district this is generally an expensive fruit to do, and is therefore not so much seen in the market. In the Midlands cherries are sold by the "side," and "half side" which represent about 60 lb. and 30 lbs. A side costs anything from 12s. to 18s., according to the amount of fruit in the market and the season. Morello cherries may be bottled according to either of the foregoing recipes.

*Raspberries and Red Currants.*—Raspberries and currants together make one of the very best fruits for winter use. They are always liked, and as they keep

# BOTTLING SOFT FRUIT

their colour well when bottled they look appetising. Also they can generally be procured at very reasonable prices, currants from 1½d. to 2½d. per lb. and raspberries from 3d. to 4d. Discrimination should be used in the weather for bottling, and a specially dry day should be chosen for doing soft fruits, for if saturated with rain they lose their flavour, and do not keep as well as when picked on a warm dry day. The currants should be carefully picked off their stalks, and also the raspberries. Place a layer of raspberries about 1 in. thick first in the bottle, and shake gently down; then place a layer of red currants. Proceed in this manner till the bottles are filled to within an inch of the top. Fill up and proceed as in the foregoing recipes. Sterilise at 155°.

*Black Currants.*—These are an excellent fruit for this work, and command a ready sale at and good prices which will give a considerable profit. A 32-oz. bottle sells for 1s. 3d. or 1s. 6d. and the fruit can usually be bought at 2d. to 3d. per lb. therefore putting the price of the bottle at 3¼d., a profit of 6d. to 9d. is shown on each bottle.

*Syrup for Bottled Fruits.*—Sometimes it is desirable to bottle the fruit in Syrup instead of water only. The following is a good recipe: To every quart of water allow ½ lb. of the best cane sugar. Bring to the boil, and continue to boil at 212° for half an hour, taking care to skim when necessary. Pour the syrup into a vessel and keep till quite cold before pouring over the fruits.

The foregoing directions can be applied, broadly speaking, to all the soft fruits enumerated at the commencement of the chapter. The temperature also must depend upon the quality of the fruit. If young and tender 155°-160° is a usual standard. The time occupied in sterilising varies with the fruit, larger fruit—such as plums—require 25 minutes, pears 1 hour, apricots 45, peaches 45, tomatoes 30, rhubarb 20 minutes.

## BOTTLING STONE FRUIT

*Plums.*—Plums should be quite freshly gathered for bottling, and only those of a fairly good size should be used. The smaller plums can always be turned into jam. The fruit should be quite firm and not quite ripe. For all the stone fruits it is best to use the larger bottles, as with the smaller bottles the mouths are not big enough to allow the insertion of any very fine fruit. The packing of plums in the bottles is an important item, because if the fruit is not properly packed the bottles present a very ugly appearance when finished. To pack properly the fruit must be graded, and plums chosen as near of a size as possible. It is always best to make a good beginning by getting three even fruits if possible into the bottom of, say, a "De Lucca" or Atlas bottle (p. 12). When the lowest round is started properly the rest of the packing is fairly simple. The bottles should be gently shaken from side to side, and a round piece of wood with a blunt end should be used to help to slide the fruit gently into place. Great care must be taken, not on any account to break the skin. Some people prick their fruit with a steel knitting needle at the stalk end, to prevent the skin breaking, but we have serious doubts whether anything is gained by so doing. The bottles, after packing, are filled up with either water or syrup. When very large plums are used they may be cut in half with a dessert knife, and the stones extracted and cracked. The kernels may then be distributed among the fruit in the bottles.

# BOTTLING STONE FRUIT

*A French Method.*—Plums which are bottled abroad often have their skins entirely removed before they are packed in the bottles. This is done by dipping the fruit into very hot water, when it will be found that the skins may be removed without any difficulty; but it is a matter of opinion whether any object is gained by the process, because the skins of plums do not become in the least uneatable from being bottled, and as it represents a good deal more time and trouble in the preparation, they must be sold at a higher price. Moreover, when finished the appearance is not so good or appetising as when bottled with the skins on.

*Sterilising Plums.*—When placed in the steriliser the temperature should be brought up very gradually till it reaches 160°. If the plums are in good condition the temperature should rise to this point without the skin cracking, but if the fruit is at all soft 155° will be sufficient. Plums are one of the most profitable of all fruits for bottling. In the plum districts the very best may be bought during the season at from 10s. to 12s. per pot which represents about 70 lb. By the very best choice fruit we mean Victorias, Czars, and Monarchs, and these in our opinion are the best varieties for preserving. The well-known Pershore plum must not be forgotten, as it bottles admirably. Damsons can be bottled in the same way.

*Apricots, Peaches, and Nectarines.*—These fruits, unless quite small, should be cut into halves, always remembering to use a dessert knife, as a steel knife will not only make the fruit taste but mark it and turn it brown or black. The stones should be cracked, and some of the kernels placed amongst the fruit when packing. The packing of the fruit is a slightly difficult operation. The halves should over-lap each other evenly up the sides of the bottles, no spaces being left. Before trying packing of this sort it would be well to purchase a properly-packed bottle and use it as a model. Care must be taken that all the juice which the fruit loses when it is being cut is saved and put into the bottles with the kernels. This can be done by halving the fruit on a plate. As apricots, peaches, and nectarines are generally expensive in this country they are not so much used for bottling, though they are very delicious, and for those who have gardens they are quite worth doing. When these fruits are in season, they come in with a rush, and the market is glutted, in consequence people do not even have the fruit gathered; as there is no sale for them raw, this is the time for bottling. All the foregoing being choice fruits, syrup may be used in the bottling instead of water. When used the fruit must not be ripe, but quite firm. Care must be taken not to bruise it when placing in the bottles. Bring them gradually up to a temperature of 155°, following in all cases the general directions for bottling.

BOTTLED FRUIT IN STORE

### BOTTLING VARIOUS FRUITS AND VEGETABLES

BESIDES soft fruits and stone fruits, there are other varieties which do not lend themselves readily for classification, *e.g.*, apples, pears, tomatoes, strawberries, etc.

The bottling of vegetables has hardly been touched upon in England yet, but we feel sure that there is a great future for this branch. Let us quote again from *The Transition of Agriculture*. This time Mr Pratt is advocating the bottling of asparagus.

"The further question is being seriously discussed at Evesham whether the ordinary markets of the country, as an outlet for fresh fruit and vegetables, could not be supplemented by the organisation of a substantial canning business which would not only utilise any possible surplus, but also substitute an important British industry for a large proportion of those canned fruits and vegetables now coming into the United Kingdom in such large quantities from other countries. It is especially pointed out that since the imposition of a duty on tinned fruit, equal to about 2s. per dozen 3-lb. tins, English fruit growers have been placed in a much better position in regard to the utilisation of their surplus produce, so much so that two years ago one firm in this country turned out in the course of the season no fewer than 1,000,000 cans of fruit. Other firms have since taken up the enterprise, which the Evesham growers expect will develop before long into a business of considerable importance, with wide possibilities of an export as well as of a home trade. In any case it should afford a *better alternation in times of 'glut'* than that of allowing plums or other fruit *to rot on the trees* because, with the *extreme lowness* of *market prices*, it will not *pay* to pluck them."

With regard to vegetables, and especially asparagus, Mr Pratt mentions on p. 141 the enormous increase of production, now covering an extent of between 3000 and 4000 acres in the Evesham district; he then continues: " The production could be extended over thousands of acres more if the surplus, after the ordinary markets had been supplied, were tinned, and either sold at home—in place of that coming in the same form from France and Germany—or else exported to our colonies or foreign countries."

The writer then shows that in the United States there are 20,000 fruit and vegetable canning factories, "*giving direct employment* to 1,000,000 persons, and indirect employment (in the way of making tins, printing labels, etc.) to 4,000,000 others." The acreage devoted to the production of these fruits and vegetables is 1,500,000 acres, divided between 30,000 farms, representing in monetary value over £6,000,000, with an output of 600,000,000 cans in a season.

Of course if we could introduce a big industry of that kind, in other places, as well as in the " Vale of Evesham," it would mean an enormous increase in the demand for labour, for which good wages could be paid, and would act as a most practical inducement to come " back to the land," or better still, for boys and youths to grow up and stay on it.

And it is no impossible chimera we are suggesting, but a thoroughly sound practical means of livelihood and prosperity.

*Apples and pears* must be carefully and evenly peeled before bottling. They should be cut down the middle as already advised for peaches, etc., removing the cores.

AN EXHIBIT OF BOTTLED FRUIT AND JAM

# BOTTLING VARIOUS FRUITS

Have ready a basin of water, into which some lemon juice has been squeezed; drop the fruit into this, and then fill the bottles with the fruit so prepared, and at once add the water or syrup. If there is any delay the fruit will turn brown, and it is to prevent this happening that it is dropped into the basin of water, the lemon juice keeping it white.

*Tomatoes* may be taken either as fruit or vegetable. Generally they come under the head of the latter, but as either they are most excellent bottled. They require a little more trouble than most other fruits to bottle successfully. They should be used small, and just coloured, as they have to be done at a high temperature, in order to insure complete sterilisation. In places where tomatoes are grown in quantities the small ones are often reserved for bottling. Pack in bottles as directed for plums, and cover with water. Bring the temperature up to 170°. Take out of the steriliser after an hour at this temperature, and leave for 24 hours; then repeat sterilisation at 170. Again leave for two or three days, and again sterilise at the same temperature. By doing them thus three times they will remain like fresh fruit, and can be kept for any length of time.

*Strawberries.*—When mentioning the soft fruits strawberries were omitted. Of all the soft fruits strawberries are the only ones that are really difficult. To the uninitiated strawberries are always a disappointment. When the bottles are taken out of the steriliser they present the appearance of a quarter of a bottle of strawberries floating at the top of a sea of juice. The only way to overcome this is to empty the contents of one bottle into another after sterilising. When one bottle is full, fill with syrup, and sterilise again. This fruit loses its colour very much during the process, takes a lot of trouble to do, and is rather insipid when done.

## FRUIT BOTTLING

THERE is nothing really mysterious about bottling. It is merely a case of sterilizing the fruit and then excluding the air by providing a vacuum. Fruit can be sterilized at much lower temperatures than vegetables because of the acids they contain which help in the process of killing the bacteria.

It is always best to use special bottles for the purpose, though latterly special caps and clips with rubber rings have been manufactured which fit perfectly to any 2-lb jam jar. These Snap Closures as they are called may be obtained from any hardware merchant or similar stores.

The true vacuum bottle should withstand the heat of sterilization and have a metal or glass lid. A new rubber ring should be used each year and this acts as a washer between the lid and the container.

## FRUIT BOTTLING

A spring clip or screw band should be provided which holds the lid in position during the heating process and during the time the fruit cools off afterwards.

All kinds of bottles can be obtained, some made of green glass, others of clear glass, some which contain 1-lb of fruit, and some as large as will contain 7-lb.

It is most important that the rim on which the lid or cap rests should not be chipped or damaged in any way, for the air might enter through this. The rim of the lid should also be perfect and must be without flaw. The rubber ring (as has already been said) must be a new one and must not contain any flaws either.

### CHOOSING THE FRUIT

For bottling, choose fruit that is free from blemish and sound. It should be just ripe and still quite firm. Try and bottle as soon after picking as possible. Grade the fruit into sizes, placing the small fruits in one bottle and the larger ones in another. This ensures greater economy of bottles for the fruit fits in better that way.

Do not attempt to bottle over-ripe or

blemished fruit. This should be made into jam or jelly.

Some fruits, like yellow egg plums and gooseberries, may be bottled on the unripe side. Some fruits, like pears, may have to be picked unripe and then be ripened on a shelf in a cool room for 2 or 3 weeks until in the right condition. It is never wise to attempt to bottle pears when they are hard.

## FRUIT PREPARATION

Always be prepared to wash fruit in plenty of cold water to make certain that it is clean. This is especially necessary when it is bought, or when it is grown in a smoky district. It is seldom necessary, however, to wash soft fruit. This should, on the other hand, be picked over carefully so as to remove any poor, unripe, or undeveloped specimens.

Soft fruit will, on the other hand, need special preparation. There is the topping and tailing of gooseberries. The stalking and plugging of raspberries, the stalking of red and black currants, etc. Sometimes it is necessary in the case of loganberries and blackberries to steep them overnight in salt and water in order to cause the maggots to come to the surface. At least an ounce of salt should be used per gallon of water.

The bottles should be washed well in warm water and should then be rinsed in clean cold water and left standing upside down until ready to use. When the bottles are moist on the inside it will be found easier to pack the fruit into the bottle for it slips into the right position more easily.

The nearer the fruits are in size the one to the other per bottle, the easier it is to pack them in tightly and the greater the quantity that can be got in.

Once all the fruit has been packed firmly (and it is surprising how many more layers can be got in after you think the bottle is full) cold water should be poured into the bottle and should be emptied out afterwards by holding the fingers across the mouth to prevent the fruit from falling out. It is possible to obtain special perforated discs which can be placed on the mouth of the bottle when it is held upside down to drain the water away. This rinsing, as it is called, is one of the refinements of good bottling and is of course not vital to its success.

## BOTTLING—THE CHEAPEST METHOD

Many women do not want to buy special jars for bottling purposes, nor do they want to purchase special vacuum closure tops with the springs and rubber rings, though these, as has already been said, are inexpensive.

Bottling in ordinary jam jars is quite a simple process without special clips or tops. The jam jar should be placed upside down on a sheet of paper placed on the oven shelf. The oven need not be hot and in fact those with a Regulo should set it at o or 1. As many jars as possible may be put in the open at a time. An hour or so later when the jars are warm. they may be taken out 2 or 3 at a time to be filled as quickly as possible with the fruit. This should be piled right up so that it even appears over the top of the rim of the bottles. They should then be put back in the oven and directly the fruit starts to shrink a patty tin may be placed over the top of each bottle so as to prevent the top layer of fruit from becoming baked. Where sufficient patty tins are not available it is usually possible to put a baking sheet or tin over all the bottles at a time.

## FRUIT BOTTLING

If the Regulo is now set at 3, or in the case of those without Regulo, if the oven door is kept closed, and the heat is a little greater, the fruit should have shrunk down to the shoulder of the bottle at the end of ¾ hour or 1 hour.

The bottles are then ready to come out one at a time. It is most important that they should be taken out of the oven to be filled with boiling *syrup one at a time*, as otherwise the heat is lost and the jar may not be properly sterilized. The hot jam jar should always be placed on a dry wooden table or on a dry cloth placed on an enamelled table.

While the jars are in the oven a syrup should be prepared consisting of ½ lb. sugar to 1 pint of water, though in war time when sugar is so scarce boiling water may be used alone. The advantage, however, of using sugar at the time of bottling is that you save approximately twice the amount of sugar when serving the fruit later.

Fill the hot jars containing the fruit with the boiling syrup so that it covers the fruit and is just above the shoulder of the bottle. Do not fill any higher than this. Be sure to cover each bottle over one at a time, so deal with the one bottle before you bring the next one out of the oven. It is important to cover over while the steam is present over the top of the syrup for this it is that is excluding the air and so will be the cause of the vacuum that is vitally needed when the fruit has cooled down.

Various materials are used for covering over the bottles. In the country pig's bladders are often prepared specially for the purpose, being of a leathery texture these are tied down and then are pasted over with a thick flour paste. Some prefer to use a piece of calico which has been dipped into a thick rice starch. This should be cut to the right size first of all, so that when it is put over it overlaps the top well, and fits snugly round the neck. When placed over, it should be pressed down tightly, squeezing the edges with the two hands and turning the bottle round from time to time.

The simplest method of all is what is known as the Three Paper method. Pieces of paper should be cut so that they overlap the rim of the jam jars about $\frac{1}{2}$ inch. Any paper will do, with the exception, of course, of very thin paper like tissue paper, blotting paper, or paper that is over thick. Paste the first disc of paper prepared with a thick flour and water paste and press it over the top of the bottle so that it overlaps $\frac{1}{2}$ inch or so all round. Then paste the top of the paper with some more of the thick flour paste. Place the next disc of paper into position, (this time newspaper will do quite well and acts as a sort of buffer) and press this down firmly, turning the bottle all the time. When firmly stuck and in position, paste the top over well once more with a thick flour paste and press the third piece of paper into position over the top. Paste this again in its turn with the thick flour paste, and then stand the bottle aside for at least an hour to dry off.

Describing this system in a book seems to take much longer than it does to do in practice. The papers can all be cut into circles beforehand and if a good brush is provided it doesn't take a minute to paint the flour paste into position.

It is surprising how effective the three pieces of paper are in acting as a seal, and there is no cheaper method known.

Whatever method is adopted to seal the jam jars it is necessary to store the bottles in a dry airy place. A hot cupboard is not really suitable nor a damp one. The best place is a shelf in the kitchen or in a passage.

Do not be tempted to lift the bottles down

from time to time to dust them, or there is a danger that they will be tipped even ever so slightly sideways and then the fruit juice or sugar solution will come into contact with the calico or paper and so cause it to rot away or let in air.

It mustn't be expected that fruit bottled in this way will keep for certain much later than the new year. Sometimes it does, of course, without any trouble at all, but the object of this simple method of bottling is really to keep fruit until, say, the middle of January. Those who want to keep it longer than this should undertake what is called the Scientific Method.

Just one or two more hints. (1) Be sure not to let mice or rats nibble the starched calico or paper. They are apt to do this if they get the chance. (2) With soft fruits it is better to pour the fruits of one bottle into another when taking them out of the oven, for they shrink so much. (3) Fruits that are particularly suitable for bottling by this method are damsons, cherries, gooseberries, plums and rhubarb. (I have included rhubarb, though of course it is really a stem and not a fruit.)

## THE SCIENTIFIC BOTTLING METHOD

Though this method has been headed "scientific" it is by no means difficult to carry out. It is a method, too, which gives perfect results. It does, however, entail the purchasing of vacuum bottles.

These are merely glass containers which have metal or glass lids. A flat or round rubber ring is used to act as a washer between the containers and the lids. Clips of a spring type or large screw bands are provided to hold the lid firmly in position during the process of sterilization. They also keep the top down tightly and thus prevent the air entering. Bottles may be bought in all sizes, usually 1 lb., 2 lb., 3 lbs. and 7 lbs.

There is no need for the bottles to be clear glass, unless, of course, you are going in for showing. On the whole small-sized bottles are best for soft fruit, and the wider-mouthed jars for apples, pears, plums, etc.

Always make certain before using the bottles that the rim around the top is not cracked or chipped. The rubber ring rests on rim this and if there is any chip the air will enter and make correct sterilization impossible.

The rubber rings should always be new ones for they deteriorate when more than a year old. They should be scalded in hot water so that any precipitated chalk may be wahed off them.

The bottles should then be placed in what is known as a "sterilizer".

## THE DEEP CONTAINER FOR STERILIZING

Those who buy bottling outfits will have the necessary deep container known as the sterilizer. These can be obtained from the ironmonger or direct from George Fowler Lee of Reading.

Any deep vessel will, however, answer the purpose, such as a saucepan, a fish kettle or even the copper used for boiling clothes. It should be deep enough in fact so that when the bottles are in it they are completely covered by the water.

Purchased sterilizers have perforated false bottoms to them which allow the water to circulate underneath the bottles and prevent them, therefore from resting on the bottom of the container. This prevents any danger of the bottles cracking. It is quite simple in the saucepan or fish kettle to put in strips of slatted wood on the bottom of the vessel first of all and place the bottles on these.

## USING A THERMOMETER

It is necessary to use a thermometer in order to find out the actual temperature. Dairy thermometers can usually be bought for 3/- or 4/-, care being taken before purchasing them to see that they will register up to 218 or 240 degrees F. Floating thermometers are ideal because when placed in the water they never disappear.

## FRUIT PREPARATION

Get the fruit ready as advised on **page 138**. Pack it tightly in the bottles and then fill up with cold syrup or cold water. It is always better to use syrup, for sugar used at bottling time saves twice the amount of sugar afterwards.

Normal Formula—1 lb. sugar to 2 pints water.

Pour this syrup into each jar until $\frac{1}{8}$ inch from top.

Having put in the syrup or water, put the

rubber ring in place, put on the lid and then fix into position the clip or clips, or screw bands. When a screw band is used it has to be screwed down firmly and then unscrewed half a turn. This is so that the air can escape while the bottles are in the sterilizer. Nothing has to be done to the clips for they give sufficiently to allow air to escape and then spring back into position again to keep the tops down tightly.

With the tops and clips in position the bottles should be placed in the sterilizer or deep vessel and brought up slowly to the right temperature. The Chart shows this quite clearly. They should then be left at that temperature for the correct time and at the end of the period should be removed one at a time, those with the screw tops being screwed down firmly. The bottles should be stood upright for 3 minutes on a wooden table and may then be laid on their sides until they are quite cold. The advantage of laying them on their sides is that this prevents the fruit from rising to the top.

When the bottles are perfectly cold examine them by removing the clips or screw tops. It should be impossible to pull off the metal or glass tops with the fingers. The bottles may then be placed on a shelf without their screw tops or clips, and if wrapped in paper, particularly blue paper, the fruit keeps a better colour.

Always try and store in a dry place for if the bottles get damp moulds may grow on the rubber rings, inwards into the bottles.

The clips and screw tops may then be given an oiling or vaselining and be put away until they are required next year. This prevents them from going rusty.

Should any of the bottles not be sealed properly, i.e., the tops come off when tried—then new rubber rings should be used and the bottles put back into the sterilizer. the process being repeated once more.

## STERILIZING CHART

| Name of Fruit | Temperature necessary | Taking 1½hrs. to reach that temperature and remaining at that temperature for |
|---|---|---|
| Apples | 165° F. | 20 mins. |
| Blackberries | 165° ,, | 20 mins. |
| Damsons | 165° ,, | 10 mins. |
| Gooseberries | 165° ,, | 10 mins. |
| Raspberries | 165° ,, | 10 mins. |
| Loganberries | 165° ,, | 10 mins. |

| Name of Fruit | Temperature necessary | Taking 1½hrs. to reach that temperature and remaining at that temperature for |
|---|---|---|
| Plums | 165° F. | 10 mins. |
| Rhubarb | 170° ,, | 15 mins. |
| Pears | 190° ,, | 30 mins. |
| Cherries | 190° ,, | 30 mins. |
| Currants | 180° ,, | 20 mins. |
| Plums, stoned | 190° ,, | 20 mins. |

It is important to take 1½ hours to reach the particular temperature in question and to ensure that the fruit remains at that temperature for the period stated.

## SPECIAL NOTES

SOFT FRUITS—

*Blackberries*—The fruit must be ripe and yet firm.

*Blackcurrants*—Use twice as much sugar as for other fruits if you wish to keep the colour.

*Red currants*—See black currants.

*Gooseberries*—Use unripe gooseberries and little sugar. ¼ lb. per pint of water is ample. If syrup is too thick the fruits shrivel. If no sugar is used the flavour is poor.

*Raspberries*—Bottle the same day as picked. Pick straight into bottles if possible. Fruit loses colour easily so wrap bottles well before storing.

*Loganberries*—Apt to be maggoty unless Derris has been used as advised in chapter on growing this fruit. Where there are maggots, soak fruit for 3 hours in salt solution. Formula—1 ounce of salt to 1 gall. water.

STONE FRUITS—

*Cherries*—Sour cherries do best. More can be got into a bottle if the fruit is stoned before using. Cheap hand-stoners may be got for this purpose from the ironmonger or direct from George Fowler Lee of Reading.

*Damsons*—Dip for 2 minutes in boiling water before putting into bottles. The sticky "bloom" is thus removed.

*Plums*—If stoned and halved before packing, twice the quantity can be got into a bottle. In this case 2 lbs. of sugar should be used per 1 quart.

POT FRUITS—

*Apples*—Peel in salted water and stand the

prepared fruit in the brine solution till ready to bottle.

Formula—2 oz. salt to 1 gall. water.

Dip the fruit for 4 minutes in boiling water before packing in bottles and then the flesh is softened and fits better into position. It is better to cut in fairly thin slices. Add a few drops of cinnamon essence to the sugar and the bottled apples will be particularly delicious.

*Pears*—Never attempt to bottle pears until they are almost fully ripe. Prepare as advised for apples. When cooking pears are bottled they must be dipped in boiling water for 4 minutes beforehand as advised in the case of apples, cut into fairly thin slices.

## PRESERVING FRUIT WITHOUT COOKING

It is possible to preserve fruit for several months without cooking or sterilizing. All that has to be done is to wash the jam jars to be used carefully, and prepare the fruit in the normal way.

The fruit should then be placed uncooked into the jam jar, and the Campden solution poured over until all the fruit is covered.

## FRUIT BOTTLING

The jar should then be sealed, preferably with a cork that can be waxed over, or by the use of a glass stopper. No metal should come into contact with this solution.

It is possible to use the three pieces of paper method as advised in the Easy Bottling Method, providing that plenty of flour paste is used to seal the pores in the paper.

To make the Campden solution it is necessary to purchase Campden tablets from the chemist. One tablet should be dissolved in ½ pint of water and this is sufficient for preserving 1 lb. of fruit.

Fruit preserved in this way is not suitable for re-sale, or for use, until it has been cooked.

This scheme has been devised by the Chipping Campden Research Station.

# Home-bottled Fruits
. and .
## How to do them.

THE bottling of fruit at home is to a very great extent of recent introduction, and even yet it has not passed its infantine stage. It is, however, an art that will rapidly grow and develop, when its possibilities are understood, and within the next year or two, we shall be greatly mistaken if up-to-date Horticultural Societies do not introduce into their schedules classes for the display of Home-bottled Fruits. Such classes would by no means be the least attractive features of the shows, and further, the Societies that interest themselves in this question by providing prizes for such produce will be doing a good work for fruit-growing at home. Bottling provides an excellent means of using surplus fruit, and further than that bottled fruit will be likely to a certain extent to take the place of jam, for if carefully prepared it is possible to have delicious fruit all the year round, and that at a very small cost.

It is a very simple undertaking to bottle fruit at home, and one which does not require any costly apparatus. To be successful, however, it is first necessary to have a good idea of the general principles governing the art, and further than that, there are a few little details—the outcome of several years' experience in fruit bottling on our part, which we shall in the course of this work describe, and which will enable anyone to undertake fruit bottling without risk of failure.

Fruit to be bottled should be as carefully selected as if it were intended for jam making, in fact, we would specially urge the importance of *using the best fruit only, and that in perfect condition.* Thinnings of trees may be used but are not recommended. As a general rule, the fruit used should be rather under ripe.

*Any fruit to be used may be first washed* and this should always be done when it is at all dusty or dirty. To wash fruit, place it in a colander and allow water from tap to swill over it thoroughly. By this means the water will drain away and thus leave fruit ready for use. There is no need for the fruit to be dried before bottling. It is best to gather soft fruits, such as raspberries, when the weather is dry, as otherwise some of the fine flavour will be lost, but as regards other fruits there is no necessity to study the weather as to when they shall be picked. Make sure that a careful selection of fruit is made and handle it as little as possible. Best of all is the fruit which can be gathered in one's own garden and used direct, but failing this make sure that a good class fruit in fresh condition is obtained. Almost all kinds of fruits may be bottled with success—gooseberries, raspberries, currants, plums, pears and many others. Different fruits require slightly different treatment, and therefore, we have dealt with the principal fruits separately. Whole fruit is bottled either in syrup or in water, and if syrup is used then the best lump sugar should be employed for that purpose, for preserving sugar often contains particles which in syrup can only be got rid of by straining.

Fruit bottles and covers should be thoroughly clean, and it is as well to rinse the bottles out with cold water before filling with fruit.

## APPARATUS.

The necessary apparatus is of the simplest kind : bottles, a thermometer, and either a pot, a large saucepan or a furnace meeting all requirements. The selection of bottles is most important.

These can often be obtained locally. They vary in price according to size and make. It is well to purchase two sizes, a small one, say 24 to 32 ounces, for soft fruits, and a larger one, say, 40 ounces, for fruits like plums. The bottles should have wide mouths and they are to be preferred if fitted with glass rather than metal lids. Metal lids rust and perish and need to be replaced every two or three years, which is not the case with glass caps. A bottle should not cost more than sixpence, and while it will be expensive to purchase a stock of bottles at this price, yet it must be borne in mind that the outlay may be regarded as capital expenditure, for with ordinary care the bottles will last year after year.* At the outside, the *average yearly cost* of a bottle should be less than a penny. This is an important point to consider, and therefore, when

---

*Prices of best English made bottles with glass tops will be sent on application. G. W. S. Brewer, Nailsworth.

bottles are required the very best obtainable should be purchased—they will prove cheapest in the end.

The essential of any bottle is, that it can be made perfectly air-tight. [It may be that a stock of bottles is already in hand and that it is desired to still use these. It is a matter of difficulty to make these perfectly air-tight even if good strong corks be used and these well driven in and sealed with paraffin wax or a mixture of Stockholm pitch and resin. We have, however, been fairly successful in the use of bladder. The bottles are first tied down with bladder and then placed in the cooking vessel, and when the contents are sufficiently sterilised, they are tied down again, as tightly as possible, with a second piece of bladder over the first. However, if the yearly cost of new corks, and wax or bladder, be considered it will be found that the patent bottles are by far the more economical.] We therefore advise the discarding of sweet bottles, etc., for the results, no matter how carefully the operations have been performed, will in most cases prove unsatisfactory. We shall be pleased to give further advice if any difficulty in procuring suitable bottles is experienced.

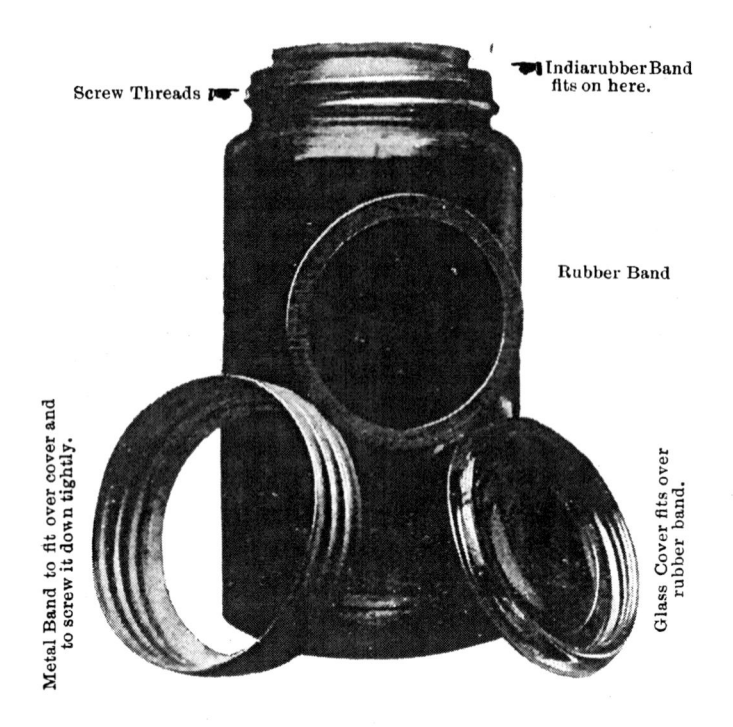

EMPTY BOTTLE SHOWING PARTS.

BOTTLES.—While then it is not absolutely essential to have special bottles for bottling purposes, yet it is very much better to have these, as by their use the ease and certainty with which the process can be conducted are strong points in favour of their employment. As pointed out previously, the cost is only one of a first outlay. Different makes of bottles vary somewhat, but the principle is practically the same in all. The bottle has on its neck threads upon which a metal cap or ring can be screwed or otherwise fastened. A metal or glass cap is used to cover the top, and this fits upon an india-rubber ring which is placed on a ledge near the top of the bottle. A metal screw band or a strong spring clip is used to hold the cap tightly in position when the sterilizing process is completed and until the covers are secure. This should make the bottle air-tight, so that no air can enter the bottle.

We can now explain the reason of the process. The contents of the bottle are heated to a certain temperature, and the cover of the bottle is only loosely fastened in position. The heat causes all the air (containing germs that cause decay) that may be in the bottle to be driven out, and its place is taken by steam and fruit vapour. Now, if the cover is securely fastened down while the temperature is high, then air (with germs) cannot enter. The bottle is allowed to cool gradually, and this causes the steam and fruit vapour which fills the space between the top of the liquid and the cover to condense into water and fruit syrup. Thus an *empty space* or *vacuum* is formed between the top of the contents of the bottle and the lid. Now Nature abhors a vacuum, and from all sides air presses firmly down on the cover in its endeavour to get inside, with the result that the lid is kept in position by the outside pressure of the atmosphere. When, therefore, the bottle and its contents are perfectly cold the screw band or clip may be removed and the lid should, if air-tight, remain tightly fixed upon the indiarubber ring. Here then is the reason of the whole process.

A thermometer can be obtained at any chemists for about a shilling. One with flat glass and round wood for dairy use is very suitable. A round glass thermometer weighted with bulb is a little more expensive, but it will stand steady in the cooking vessel, and that is a great advantage. If the thermometer rises in the water it can be weighted by tying a little bag of shot to the bottom. We use a zinc dairy thermometer which cost a shilling and which answers the purpose admirably. In any case have a thermometer which can be thrust or stood in hot water; and see that it is eight to nine inches long and with the figures plainly marked.

A pot, a large saucepan, or a furnace will complete the outfit, except that a wooden platform should be made on which to place the bottles during the cooking process. This wooden platform is a very simple affair and can be made at home. Two pieces of wood about half an inch to three-quarters of an inch thick will be required. Cut these roughly to the shape of the cooking vessel used and so that the two pieces when nailed together by means of two cross pieces underneath will fit into the vessel. The cross pieces will allow the platform to be raised above the bottom of the cooking vessel and will also allow of free circulation of the water. The accompanying diagram will show exactly what is required.

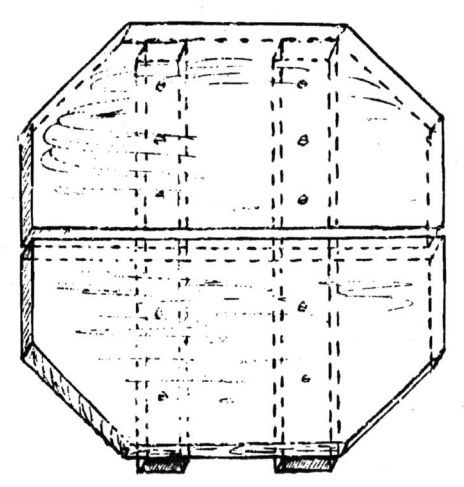

If the furnace is used then the platform should be made to stand about 6 to 8 inches off the bottom. To keep it in this position it will be necessary to tie or otherwise fasten a weight (a brick will do) underneath it to keep it in position. For an ordinary sized furnace two pieces of wood about 16 inches long and eight inches wide, nailed together with cross pieces and then the corners sawn off will do excellently. Do not let the two pieces of wood touch each other by about a quarter of an inch and then this will allow a piece of string for fastening the weight to be below the surface of the platform and so not interfere with its evenness. The bottles when ready will be placed on this wooden platform. *On no account* must the bottles stand direct on the metal of the vessel or breakages will occur. One bottle, or several, may be done at a time and the process is similar in all cases. We find that an ordinary sized furnace will accommodate about 12 bottles at a time, while a large pot will take six or seven, and a large saucepan two or three.

## GOOSEBERRIES.

Gooseberries are generally bottled when green, and they are fit for use as soon as they are *full grown, but still quite green.* Keepsake, Whinham's Industry, and other varieties are all excellent for bottling. After topping and tailing, the fruit may be placed in the bottles, which should first be rinsed out with water. From time to time as the filling proceeds the fruit should be well shaken down, and to do this knock very gently the bottom of the bottle on some solid piece of wood such as a table, taking care not to break the bottle. The after appearance of the bottle will depend very much upon the manner in which it is packed with fruit. Fill each bottle to within about an inch and a half of the top. Either syrup or water must next be poured into each bottle so as to cover the fruit. *There should be about an inch clear space between the top of the liquid and the cover* to allow for expansion of the fruit and syrup when heated. For gooseberries we always use water in preference to syrup but those who would like to use syrup may find recipe for making it on page 21. Place cover in position, and *screw on lightly only. If caps with clips are used they are fastened on and not touched until the sterilisiug is completed and the bottles quite cold.* Take pains to see that the rubber rings and caps fit perfectly. When the bottles are all ready they may be placed on the wooden platform already described, in the pot or other vessel which should be on the fire. Take care that each bottle does not quite touch either of its neighbours. If this is done the packing with hay or cloths may be entirely dispensed with. Next pour in *cold* water as high as the vessel will allow, but not higher than the bases of the necks of the bottles. Stand the thermometer in the vessel. The water should be *gradually* heated until a temperature of about 160 degrees Fahrenheit is reached. On the slow, even, and gentle rise of the temperature will depend much of the success in obtaining fruit with uncracked skins. This part of the sterilising ought to take about an hour, but if the temperature has been reached in much less time than an hour, it is better to keep at 160 degrees for about 10 minutes, or else to further raise the temperature of the water until 165 degrees are reached, so as to ensure the contents of the bottles being at the same temperature as the water of the vessel. If the vessel is on a fire, lift it off carefully, after having first removed the bottles. If a furnace is used rake out the fire. If gas or oil is the heating agent then turn it off. Each bottle should now have its cover securely fastened down, and then be replaced in the vessel and allowed to cool gradually. While the cooling is taking place the lids may once or twice be examined, and if necessary further tightened. *By-the-bye, always take the precaution to wrap a cloth or duster round each bottle when handling it while hot, and especially when fastening down lid.* It is possible a bottle may crack, and the cloth in such a case would prevent harm from splinters of glass. We may remark, however, that in the hundreds of bottles we have prepared we have never had a bottle burst; but still, accidents of this kind may arise, and it is as well to be safeguarded. When the bottles are *perfectly cold* unscrew the metal bands where this type of bottle is used, or remove the clips, and if perfectly airtight then the lid will be quite fast upon the rubber ring. Before replacing the screw bands wipe carefully the threads of the bottles and bands and smear a little vaseline on them. If this is not done then a little syrup may be on the bands, and hence when the fruit is required for use the bands may be found stuck and difficult to remove.

In the event of a bottle not proving air-tight, it should be again placed in a vessel of cold water with the top lightly screwed on and heated as before, and when quite cold be again tested. It may be, on rare occasions, that even a third attempt may be necessary, but this does not often happen if the above directions have been carefully followed, especially bearing in mind that the bottles are not to be tested until *quite cold*. The bottles are then stored away upright, and the contents may be used in like manner to green gooseberries fresh from the garden.

Ripe gooseberries are generally eaten uncooked, and it is not advisable to bottle when in this state.

## RASPBERRIES.

Raspberries should not be dead ripe when picked for bottling, and yet they should be sufficiently ripe to be firm and to part readily from the cores. It is often an advantage to pick the raspberries direct into the bottles and thus save handling as much as possible. If this is done, care must be taken to avoid fragments of leaves, etc., from falling into the bottles and thus spoiling their appearance. Raspberries are often disfigured by grubs and frequently grubs are found in the raspberries. If such is the case they should be carefully looked over before being bottled. Shake fruit well down from time to time as the filling proceeds and fill each bottle to within about an inch and a half of the top. We recommend raspberries, a sweet fruit, to be always bottled in syrup, and this may be made according to instructions below. When the bottles have been thus filled and either water or syrup added so as to just cover the fruit, screw the caps on lightly or place caps and clips in position, and treat as described for gooseberries.

We find, however, that these do better if raised to about 155 degrees, and then are allowed to remain at this temperature for about 10 to 15 minutes before they are securely fastened down. The aim should be to have each raspberry whole when the operation is completed.

*Raspberries and Red Currants*, or *Raspberries and Black Currants* may be bottled together, and so treated are excellent for serving as stewed fruits with Custard or Blanc Mange or for making into tarts and puddings.

## SYRUP.

For each pint of water allow about ¼lb. best lump sugar. Put into a suitable vessel on the fire, and stir till sugar is dissolved. Boil for about 10 minutes taking off any scum that may appear. Set this solution on one side to cool and when cold the syrup may be put into the bottles of fruit. It is quite as economical, if not more so, to bottle fruit in syrup than in water, for, whenever the fruit is to be used sugar must be added. If syrup is used in bottling it helps considerably to retain the flavour and appearance of the fruit. Most fruits bottled in water are flavourless and of poor colour. With slight variations this syrup will answer for practically all fruits.

## CURRANTS.

Currants need to be carefully picked so that as far as possible each fruit may remain whole. This is hardly attainable when the fruit is hurriedly stripped off the bushes. If a bottle is required for exhibition purposes it may be as well to pick the currants in bunches and then cut each fruit off separately with a pair of scissors. This of course takes much longer and is not necessary for household purposes. Currants may, if clean, be picked direct into the bottles, care of course being taken to let no foreign matter enter the bottles. Fill the bottles and treat exactly as recommended for raspberries. Currants answer very well, especially black currants, if done in water. Personally, we prefer them prepared in syrup.

*Black Currants and Rhubarb* form an excellent mixture. Use three parts of black currants to one part of rhubarb. First wash rhubarb, then skin and cut into pieces about 2 inches long. The pieces may be put in here and there with the currants.

## STRAWBERRIES.

As strawberries are generally eaten uncooked this fruit does not form a good subject for bottling either regarded from the standpoint of flavour, appearance or usefulness. If required they should be carefully selected when the berries are ripe but still nice and firm—small fruit is better than large. They should be bottled in syrup made slightly heavier than that for raspberries. Bottle and sterilise exactly as recommended for raspberries. Store in a dark cupboard or the colour of the fruit will fade. Strawberries may be bottled in a syrup made by boiling one pint of red currant juice (in place of water) with each half pound of sugar. This is said to greatly improve flavour and appearance.

## LOGANBERRIES.

This fruit is gradually coming into common use. It has a distinct flavour of its own and may not on that account suit all palates. Loganberries should be bottled in syrup, heated to a temperature of 160 degrees, and kept at that temperature for at least ten minutes, before being tightly fastened down.

## MORELLO CHERRIES.

Morello Cherries may be bottled whole in syrup. They should be heated to about 165 degrees, and allowed to remain at this temperature for about 10 minutes. Some prefer to stone them before bottling.

## PLUMS.

The plum family is certainly the most popular and profitable for bottling purposes It is, as a rule, the cheapest fruit to purchase and where one has plum trees they often bear abundantly, and as the plum season is very brief they must be used up quickly. Bottling then comes in very useful.

For bottling purposes one of the finest plums is the yellow plum, known as the Pershore. It can often be purchased at less than a penny a pound so that a bottle can be filled for about twopence. It should be picked when still green, but yet just on the point of becoming ripe. The plums should be carefully packed in the bottles and the handle of a wooden jam spoon is often useful to make a refractory plum fit just into its right place. Shake the plums well down into the bottles and fill with syrup to within about an inch of the top. Unless the plums are well packed in the bottles before the syrup is added it will be found that after sterilising, the fruit will stand some way up the bottle and thus somewhat spoil the appearance. In packing, guard against bruising or cracking the fruit. If any fruits are a little cracked or otherwise disfigured, then place in the bottle with best side outwards. Plums should be slowly raised to a temperature of 165 degrees. If the fruit is very ripe only allow the temperature to reach 160 degrees. Keep at the required temperature for about 15 minutes before firmly screwing down.

Pershore plums, if carefully done, are of a lovely golden colour and their flavour is delicious.

Victoria plums is another favourite bottling subject. Medium sized fruit should be selected. Bottle in syrup and treat like Pershore plums.

Greengage, Czar, Monarch, and other plums may be similarly bottled. Goliath, with peach-like flavour, is an excellent plum for this purpose.

Plums may also be bottled by another method. Instead of placing fruit in bottles and sterilising, it may be placed in bulk in an enamelled pan, covered with syrup and brought to a temperature not exceeding 180 degrees and kept at this temperature for a few minutes only, if necessary. Meanwhile the bottles should be warmed by having some hot water (not boiling) poured into them and afterwards emptied, or they may be warmed in an oven. The rubbers should also be put into hot water and warmed.

When the plums, still whole, are sufficiently cooked they should be most carefully ladled into the bottles. The difficulty in doing this is to keep the plums whole. Fill bottles nearly full with syrup, and fasten down immediately. Bottles done by this method can be more closely packed with fruit, but there is much more danger of the fruit being broken than if the plums are cooked in the bottles separately. When cold the bottles should be tested, and if not air-tight they should be placed in a cooking vessel on the wooden platform, and raised to a temperature of 160 degrees, and then screwed down firmly again. This method of bottling can be employed where large quantities are to be done, as it can be performed very much quicker than when the sterilising is done in the bottles. We much prefer the other method.

## DAMSONS.

Damsons are, if anything, the easiest and most satisfactory of all fruits for bottling. For one thing their size allows them to lie closely together, and thus they can be well packed in the bottles. They should be done in syrup and treated as recommended for plums.

## PEARS.

Pears are excellent when bottled, and they may be done at home equal, if not superior to the Californian bottled fruits now on the English market. First, a good pear for stewing should be obtained. Windsor or Catillac, as well as others, are excellent varieties. Pears to be bottled should be prepared exactly as if they are to be dished up and served at table as stewed pears (see next page), and when in this state the fruit should be placed in warm bottles. Warm the rubbers also. Fill each bottle with syrup to within about an inch of the top and immediately fasten the lid securely. When quite cold test to see if air-tight. If not, the bottle with fruit in should, with its covering *lightly* screwed on, be placed on platform in a vessel of water and heated to 160 degrees and then the cover again made secure. When quite cold, test again.

*Recipe for Stewing Pears for Bottling.*

Prepare a syrup, by using half-a-pound of best lump sugar to each pint of water. [By some, stewed pears are preferred when flavoured; and this can be done by putting lemon juice, spice, ginger, wine, etc., into the syrup.]

Each pear should be peeled, cut into halves, cored and immediately placed in the syrup to prevent discolouration. When ready, place the vessel on the fire and bring to the boil and then allow the pears to *simmer gently* until they can be easily pierced with a needle. Care should be taken that they are not allowed to break. Thus prepared they are ready for bottling according to the instructions already given.

[If fruit is required of a deep pink colour this may be obtained by adding a few drops of cochineal or a small quantity of red currant juice, shortly before removing from the fire.]

## APPLES.

As apples may now be obtained nearly all the year round there is not the need for bottling this fruit as exists in other cases.

It may be, however, that some may wish to bottle a portion of their own surplus crop of apples. If so, prepare in the same manner as recommended for pears, taking care to watch the apples carefully, as unlike pears some apples tend to cook to a pulp. Apples and mulberries together bottle very well and are nice for tarts or as stewed fruit. Apples and Blackberries, too, is another good mixture.

## BLACKBERRIES.

This favourite fruit can generally be obtained in abundance in the country in Autumn while town dwellers can buy it very cheaply. Blackberries alone are rather inclined to be "seedy" and therefore it is perhaps better to bottle them with apples. Where, however, it is wished to bottle this fruit, follow exactly the directions given for raspberries.

———:o:———

There are other fruits such as peaches, apricots, figs, etc., which may be bottled. We have, however, restricted ourselves to describing those fruits which are commonly in demand. If peaches and apricots are bottled, the fruit should be cut in halves and the stones removed. A few kernels may be added for flavour if necessary. Bottle then as recommended for plums.

———:o:———

*Cranberries, Whortleberries,* or *Billberries* are plentiful in some places and are most useful for tarts when bottled similarly to currants.

## TOMATOES.

Many persons during the season have a surplus of tomatoes and to such, a recipe for bottling should be valuable. The following will be found to answer excellently from all points of view. We use for this purpose the 2lb., size bottles which will take rather less than $1\frac{1}{2}$ lbs. of tomatoes (weighed before cooking). Select the smallest tomatoes and prick each in several places with a needle. Make a syrup using 2 ozs. sugar to a pint of water, adding a little lemon juice if preferred. Put tomatoes into this syrup and place in a double saucepan—(this should be enamelled) and heat very gradually until about 190 degrees have been reached. Give ten to twenty minutes at this temperature and they should then be sufficiently cooked, and still remain whole. By means of a wooden jam-spoon carefully fill the bottles, which have been warmed in readiness and then add syrup to within half an inch of the top. Screw down immediately. When cold test to see if bottles are airtight—if not heat the bottles as they are, on platform in cooking vessel, *with covers tightly fixed*, to 165 degrees and then take out and screw down. Care must be taken not to cook the tomatoes too much and experience will readily show just when they are quite fit. Much of course depends upon the degree of ripeness; while there may also be slight differences owing to different varieties of tomatoes.

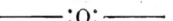

———:o:———

We have made rather a strong point of the fact that no special apparatus is required. Not every home possesses a double saucepan such as described for bottling tomatoes, but this difficulty can be readily surmounted as follows:—if an enamelled basin is at hand (one suitable can be purchased as cheaply as 6½d.) An ordinary saucepan into which the enamelled basin will fit down somewhat can be partly filled with water. The basin should then be placed in position—it should touch the water, but ought not to go right into the saucepan, and should be held in position by the sides of the saucepan.

The tomatoes should be put into the basin and covered with syrup and to hold them under the syrup a plate which will fit down into the basin may be placed bottom upwards, on the top of the tomatoes. After the water in the saucepan has boiled for say ten minutes, lift the plate by means of a knife and cloth and examine the tomatoes. If not done, cover up again for a time and then examine again. A little of the water in the saucepan cooled down somewhat, may be put into the bottles and shaken round : this will warm them ready for the tomatoes. Rubber bands may also be warmed. When tomatoes are sufficiently cooked fill into the bottles and treat as described above.

———:o:———

The instructions we have given concerning the bottling of fruit are the result of experiences gained in preparing some hundreds of bottles. It may be, however, owing to some little difference in type of bottle, in the degree of ripeness of fruit, or in rapidity or slowness at which the sterilising is done, that some slight modification of our recipes may occasionally be found necessary. Experience and common sense must then be the guide. In all general cases we are convinced that the results will be gratifying if our instructions are carefully followed.

———:o:———

For some reason (generally through not properly sterilising, a flaw in the bottle or the cap or rubber not being fitted exactly), it may happen that the contents of a bottle will ferment, and go bad. It is well, then, to occasionally look over the bottled fruits for a few weeks after placing them away, and if the syrup in a bottle shows marked signs of discolouration or " muddiness " place the bottle on one side and watch carefully. If, when the bottle is quite at rest, bubbles rise through the syrup, then the contents are fermenting. In such a case the top layers of fruit and syrup should be poured off, and probably the remaining portion may be used.

Sometimes a little of the fruit in the bottle stands above the syrup and becomes discoloured. This will not matter and when the bottle is opened the discoloured fruit may be discarded.

If the fruit rises from the bottom of the bottle and floats in the syrup it may be that the fruit was not well packed. Some fruits, gooseberries for instance, rise owing to the fruit being lighter, bulk for bulk than the syrup.

It is well to bear in mind that when fruit is bottled it should not be cooked too much—it only requires thorough scalding or sterilising, a somewhat similar operation to scalding milk.

## STORING OF FRUIT.

Bottled fruit may be stored on open shelves or in cupboards. It may be taken as a general rule that where jam can be stored, bottled fruit can similarly be kept.

Strong light will tend to make the syrup darken, while in the case of **strawberries** light will tend to bleach the fruit. Hence if fruit is exposed on open shelves or cupboards it is well to cover over with sheets of brown paper.

―――:o:―――

## OPENING OF BOTTLES.

Bottled fruit may be used at any time—a few days, a few weeks or months after being prepared. The bottles should be carefully opened so that the rubbers and covers may be used again. For screw-capped bottles remove first of all the metal bands, and then to open, the point of a penknife or scissors inserted just above or below the rubber band, and moved a little will allow the air to penetrate. The pressure of the air thus removed, the cover may be easily taken off. In case any difficulty is experienced in opening a bottle, place it in a cool oven and warm, or place it in cold water and heat. When hot the covers can generally be removed with ease. When opened, the fruit if quite soft, may be used as it is cold, if bottled in syrup, but we prefer to put it into a stew pan, adding sugar according to taste, and bringing it to the boil for a minute or so. The fruit may then be served like freshly stewed fruit, from which it will be difficult to distinguish it.

Fruit when once opened should be used within a few days as it will not keep good any more than stewed fresh fruit would do.

## USE OF FRUIT.

There is one bad mark to be scored against bottled fruit, and that is its use for Tarts, as being saturated in syrup it tends to make the pastry sodden, but good cooks will know how to overcome difficulties of this kind.

A most delicious dish which can be quickly prepared, may be made by serving the fruit with either Custard or Blanc Mange, while Cream is certainly not to be despised.

Another well-known and delightful way of using soft fruits such as Raspberries, Raspberries and Currants, or other mixed fruits, is to put the fruit into the stew pan, add a little sugar to taste, then bring to the boil. Meanwhile, line a basin with sponge cakes—a more economical way, however, and one which answers equally well, is to use slices of stale bread, without crusts, in place of the sponge cakes. Pour the hot fruit into the basin and then cover it with more cakes or slices of bread. Place a plate, weighted, over the top and set aside till cold. Turn out into a deep dish and pour over it a custard and set aside again till cold. It is better to prepare this dish the day before it is required so that the bread or cakes may be properly saturated with the syrup. This recipe is a good one from another standpoint in that it allows all the syrup to be used with the fruit.

There are of course many other ways of serving bottled fruit, and for these we

---

Alfred Bird & Sons, Birmingham (The proprietors of Bird's Custard Powder) in their book " Pastry & Sweets " give a number of recipes for using bottled fruit. They will on receipt of name and address of any reader be pleased to forward free a copy of this work.

must refer our readers to their own experiences or to their cookery books. There is often more syrup in a bottle than is needed for use with the fruit, if so, the surplus may be utilised for making fruit beverages, jellies, etc.

## EMPTY BOTTLES.

When emptied, the bottles before being stored away, should be thoroughly cleansed with scalding (not boiling) water and placed to drain. The rubbers, covers, and screw bands should also be washed and wiped quite dry.

The rubbers may be stored inside the bottles. Metal covers require to be stored in a perfectly dry place or they will rust. If it should happen that some of the rubber rings or other parts need renewing get these at once and not wait until the bottles are wanted and be disappointed in consequence. If bottles are thus carefully tended they may be used over and over again.

———:o:———

We believe there is a great future for Home-bottled fruits and we have endeavoured to show that the process is by no means a "fancy one, but is simple, sure, and reliable, where pains are taken. We do not wish bottling to be regarded as only providing a means for utilising an occasional surplus stock of fruit. We look upon it as being as indispensable to a household as the making of jams, marmalade, or pickles. Viewed in this light a dozen bottles may well form the stock for the first year and each year extra bottles may be added until a sufficient stock has been accumulated. Each must, of course, decide how many bottles will be likely to be required for use during the year. For a household of four or five persons four dozen bottles in all may prove sufficient, while six dozen may not prove any too many.

It is, of course, much the best to use fruit grown in one's own garden because it may be gathered when it is in just the fittest state of ripeness, and also the fruit may be more carefully selected, and so be free from bruises, etc. Where fruit cannot be obtained at home it is well to try and get it fresh from the growers rather than from shops, as by so doing it is likely to be subjected to less handling.

———o:o———

It may not be altogether out of place to remark that may persons grow in their gardens fruit—currants, gooseberries, apples, etc.—of very inferior sorts. This is a great mistake, for the same land and culture would serve to grow the best varieties. It is better, then, where inferior fruit is grown to gradually root up the poor varieties and replace with new stocks which can be relied upon to produce the finest and best fruit. Any nurseryman of repute will be pleased to advise on a choice of suitable fruit stock.

———o:o———

The bottling of vegetables we have not entered upon except in the case of tomatoes and chiefly for the reason that vegetables are fairly plentiful all the year round and only in one or two instances—peas, kidney beans, asparagus—are they suitable for bottling. They require different treatment altogether from fruit.

———:o:———

We would again impress the importance of using sound fruit in perfect condition, and also to make sure that strict cleanliness is observed in regard to fruit and all utensils used—bottles and parts. No preservatives whatever are used, with the exception of sugar, nor are any required. Bottled fruit should, if required, keep for years.

———:o:———

The writer will be pleased at any time to give, as far as he can, further information on any points that may be desired in connection with this subject, while at the same time he will be thankful to receive any corrections or suggestions for the improvement of the book.

In using a pot or furnace as a sterilising vessel it is necessary to see that the water reaches well up to the necks of the bottles and the vessel should have a cover put over it. If a cover is not used it may be found that, after storing, some of the fruit (plums especially liable owing to their thickness) at the top of the bottle turns discoloured owing to not having been acted upon to the same extent by the heat as the remainder.

——— : o : ———

## HOW TO UTILISE SPARE FRUIT SYRUP.

In nearly all cases of using bottled fruits it will be found that there is more or less syrup to spare, and this can be made into jellies as follows. The quantities given below are about what may be expected to be obtained from surplus syrup from a 2-lb. bottle of fruit.

Just cover ½-oz. of gelantine with cold water, and soak for about an hour. Strain the surplus syrup through a jelly bag or through muslin into a suitable saucepan. Add a little water, sufficient to make syrup up to about one pint. Sweeten with a few lumps of sugar and boil. Turn the gelantine into the boiling syrup, and stir until dissolved. Pour into a wetted mould, and place aside to set.

A correspondent has kindly furnished the following method of utilising spare fruit syrup :—" Use the sweetened fruit juice (diluted with water if too strong) *instead* of milk, and thicken with cornflour in the ordinary way. This is a regular German dish, and makes a pretty red mould with currant juice, a dark one with damson juice, etc. It is generally served with cream."

## VEGETABLES.

The bottling of vegetables is a much more difficult process to undertake than that of bottling fruit, and this is due to the chemical composition of vegetables differing from that of fruits. The vegetables usually bottled are asparagus, young carrots, peas and beans, and they should be selected when quite young and tender. The ordinary sterilising process as recommended for fruits will fail when applied to vegetables. They can, however, be bottled more or less satisfactorily by sterilising at a higher temperature than that of boiling water (212 degrees Fahrenheit). This can be accomplished either by using a special sterilising apparatus or else, where this is not available, by sterilising in a strong brine solution made by dissolving as much salt as possible in the water in the cooking vessel. The vegetables duly prepared and packed in the bottles with any seasoning or green colouring matter (in case of peas and beans) that may be required, are placed in the sterilising vessel. Do not, on any account, use copperas for colouring. Slowly raise the temperature until the highest possible point is reached, and keep at this temperature for about half-an-hour, when secure caps and let cool slowly. Next day re-sterilise again in a similar manner, and then finally secure caps. Store bottles away, and watch for some weeks to see that contents are right.

## MUSHROOMS.

Select some small mushrooms in a firm and good condition. Wash and salt, and cut off dirt. Place them in an enamelled saucepan with a little salt sprinkled over, and gradually allow juice to draw out. When this has taken place pull off the fire and let the mushrooms suck up juice again. Boil some white wine vinegar, add a little spice, and put mushrooms in while hot and then add a little syrup. Secure caps while hot.

## JELLIES.

The two following recipes may prove welcome to some:—

*Crab Apple Jelly*—Take a quantity of crabs, remove the stalks and wash them clean with plenty of water. Place the crabs in the preserving kettle, and well cover with water and simmer till quite soft. Place into jelly bag, and let juice run out (do not press bag). For each pint of juice allow a pound of preserving sugar and boil until it jellies, which should take about an hour.

*Bramble Jelly*—Place blackberries in a preserving pan, they may be first washed in a colander if necessary—add about a pint of water to each pound of blackberries, and boil until well cooked. Strain through jelly bag, and then re-boil juice, adding one pound preserving sugar to each pint of syrup. When it will jelly it is done, and this should take about an hour.

# *Bottling or Canning*

*A*S *canning or bottling to preserve food is a new development sponsored by cooker manufacturers, we are reprinting an introduction sent to us covering the famous "Presto" Cooker, which, we are sure, our readers will find of great interest should they be contemplating the processing of foods.*

## AN INTRODUCTION TO BOTTLING OR CANNING IN A "PRESTO" COOKER

Follow these simple steps in using your "PRESTO" COOKER for bottling or canning. Pressure Cooking is the only safe method for processing non-acid foods.

Use 5 lbs. pressure for bottling fruit and tomatoes. Use 10 lbs. pressure for bottling vegetables, meat, poultry, fish, etc.

### STEPS FOR BOTTLING IN A "PRESTO" COOKER

1. Use only jars in perfect condition, free from nicks, cracks and sharp edges. Wash jars and lids in hot, soapy water. Rinse thoroughly and stand in hot water until ready for use.
   The 4-quart "PRESTO" COOKER holds 4 standard 1 lb. jam jars, or 3 1 lb. Kilner jars.
   If metal lids with sealing compound are used, dip in boiling water just before use.
2. Select fresh, firm, ripe products and sort according to size and degree of ripeness.
3. Clean food thoroughly, in several waters if necessary. Lift food out of water in washing.
4. Pre-cook food according to the following directions.
5. Fill hot jars with hot food, according to directions, leaving ½" headspace for fruit and tomatoes and all other foods, and 1" headspace for vegetables, such as peas and beans.
6. Cover with hot liquid as specified in recipe.
7. Work out air bubbles with clean knife.
8. Wipe top of jar clean of all seeds, pulp and grease.
9. Adjust closures on jars according to type of jar used.
10. Place rack upside down in Cooker and pour in 2 pints boiling water.

11. Place hot jars on rack in Cooker. Turn heat on full.
12. Place cover on Cooker.
13. Allow steam to flow from vent pipe for 3 to 4 minutes.
14. Place Indicator Weight on vent pipe and process according to time given in Time Table. Start counting processing time the minute stem reaches desired level. Regulate heat to maintain pressure at required level. Fluctuations in pressure may force liquid from jar.
15. Turn off heat at end of processing time and remove Cooker from heat.
16. Let stem return to DOWN position. WHEN BOTTLING DO NOT COOL COOKER UNDER RUNNING WATER OR BY PUTTING IN A PAN OF COLD WATER, AS THIS WILL CAUSE JARS TO BURST.
17. When stem reaches DOWN position, remove Indicator Weight. Remove cover from Cooker. Tilt upper side of cover towards you to keep steam away from you.
18. Remove jars from Cooker and place on a board or towel away from draughts.
19. Tighten closures while hot—except the metal caps which seal themselves.
20. Twenty-four hours later, test seal, wipe jars clean, label and date, then store in a cool, dry place.

## BOTTLING FRUIT

Although fruit has better colour, shape and flavour when bottled with sugar, it may be successfully bottled unsweetened. Sugar is used for flavour. It is not in high enough concentration to act as a preservative. Jars should be filled to the shoulder with fruit, and then cover fruit with syrup, or boiling water to within half an inch of top of jar.

The amount of sugar required in preparing the syrup will depend on the tartness of the fruit, and on family preferences. It should be remembered that fruit when heating will release some of its juices, which will dilute the syrup in proportion to the juiciness of the fruit.

Fruit, except apples and strawberries, may be packed raw into jars and then covered with the boiling syrup or water. When this is done there is no need to increase processing time. When fruit is packed cold it shrinks and the container is less full than when pre-heated in boiling syrup before packing.

## TABLE OF SYRUPS FOR BOTTLING FRUIT

| Kind of Syrup | Sugar | Liquid-water or Juice |
|---|---|---|
| Thin | 8 oz. | 1½ pt. |
| Medium | 8 oz. | 1 pt. |
| Thick | 8 oz. | ½ pt. |

Heat sugar with liquid or juice until the sugar has dissolved. About ½ pint syrup is needed for 1 lb. jars.

Do not use saccharine as a substitute for sugar when bottling.

APPLES.—Wash, peel, and cut in quarters or slices. Place in a weak solution of brine—1½ teaspoons of salt to one quart of water—until ready for use, to prevent darkening. Drain well. Pre-cook by boiling apples in a thin syrup for 4 to 5 minutes. Pack hot apples in clean, hot jars. Cover fruit with hot syrup, in which it was cooked. Adjust lids. Process in Cooker according to Time Table.

APPLE PUREE.—Wash apples, remove spots and blemishes. Cut in halves or quarters. To each 5 lbs. of fruit add 1 pint water and cook until tender. Pass through a fine sieve, sweeten to taste. Re-heat and pack in hot, clean jars. Adjust lids. Process in Cooker according to Time Table.

APRICOTS.—Select well-ripened, but firm fruit. Wash. Dip in boiling water for one minute and then in cold water to remove skins. Remove stones if required. Pre-cook 3 to 5 minutes in boiling medium syrup. Pack in hot, clean jars. Cover with boiling syrup in which they were cooked. Adjust lids. Process in Cooker according to Time Table.

BERRIES.—Handle berries carefully to prevent crushing or bruising. Wash carefully and pick over. Put in pan and cover with syrup. Bring to boil. Shake pan to prevent berries from sticking. Pack in hot, clean jars. Cover with boiling syrup. Adjust lids. Process in Cooker according to Time Table.

CHERRIES.—Wash and stem cherries. Put cherries in pan with syrup, and bring to boil. Pack in hot, clean jars. Cover with boiling syrup. Adjust lids. Process in Cooker according to Time Table.

PEACHES.—Select well-ripened, but sound fruit. Sort according to size. Plunge in boiling water for 1 minute to loosen skins. Dip in cold water. Remove skins and stones. Leave in halves or slice. Drop into a weak solution of brine —$1\frac{1}{2}$ teaspoons salt to 1 quart of water—to prevent darkening until ready for use. Drain well. Simmer 5 to 6 minutes in medium syrup. Pack in hot, clean jars. Cover with boiling syrup. Adjust lids. Process in Cooker according to Time Table.

PEARS.—Wash and peel. Cut large pears in half and core. Place in a weak solution of brine—$1\frac{1}{2}$ teaspoons salt to 1 quart water—to prevent darkening until ready for use. Drain well. Simmer 5 to 6 minutes in medium syrup. **Pack in hot, clean jars. Cover with boiling syrup. Adjust lids.** Process in Cooker according to Time Table.

PLUMS.—Select firm, ripe fruit. Wash and remove stems. Prick skins with a fork if to be bottled whole. **Pre-cook in medium syrup for 2 to 3 minutes. Pack in hot, clean jars. Cover with boiling syrup. Adjust lids. Process in Cooker according to Time Table.

RASPBERRIES.—Select firm, but ripe fruit. Wash and remove stems. Handle carefully to prevent crushing or bruising. Pack raw in clean, hot jars. Shake down for full pack. Cover with boiling thin syrup. Adjust lids. Process in Cooker according to Time Table.

RHUBARB.—Select young and tender rhubarb—strawberry variety if possible. Wash thoroughly. Remove ends and cut in 1" lengths. Put in pan and add sugar and water, and bring slowly to boil. Pack in hot, clean jars. Cover with boiling syrup. Adjust lids. Process in Cooker according to Time Table.

**STRAWBERRIES.**—Select ripe, but firm berries. Wash, drain and hull. Put in a pan with sugar and water and bring slowly to boil. Remove from stove and allow to stand overnight. Bring quickly to boil. Pack in hot, clean jars. Cover with syrup. Adjust lids. Process in Cooker according to Time Table.

| Fruit | Pressure | Times for Glass Jars (1 lb.) in Minutes |
|---|---|---|
| Apples | 5 | 10 |
| Apple Puree | 5 | 8 |
| Apricots | 5 | 10 |
| Berries (except Strawberries) | 5 | 8 |
| Cherries | 5 | 10 |
| Peaches | 5 | 10 |
| Pears | 5 | 10 |
| Plums | 5 | 10 |
| Raspberries | 5 | 8 |
| Rhubarb | 5 | 5 |
| Strawberries | 5 | 5 |

## BOTTLING VEGETABLES.

Young, tender and fresh vegetables, slightly immature, are better for bottling than those which are over-ripe. As a rule, vegetables are better if bottled immediately after picking, since flavour decreases upon standing, and often detracting colour changes take place. Avoid bruising, because spoilage organisms grow more rapidly on bruised vegetables than on unblemished ones.

All vegetables are pre-cooked before processing. When vegetables are pre-cooked in boiling water, some of their nutrients are dissolved in the water, so, wherever possible, the pre-cooking liquid should be used as liquid to cover the vegetables, such as turnips, greens, and sometimes asparagus, which make cooking liquid bitter. Do not use cooking liquid in these cases.

Leave 1in. head space when bottling starchy vegetables such as peas and shelled beans. Half-inch head space is sufficient for all other vegetables. It is best not to use free-running salt containing starch, as it may make the liquid cloudy and the product unattractive.

ASPARAGUS.—Select young and tender asparagus. Sort according to size. Wash thoroughly, giving special attention to scales which may harbour dirt and grit from garden. Remove tough ends and larger scales. Cut in 1in. lengths, or tie in bundles. Pre-cook in boiling water for 3 minutes. Pack in hot, clean jars. Add ½ teaspoon salt to each 1 lb. jar. Cover with fresh boiling water. Adjust lids. Process according to Time Table.

FRENCH OR RUNNER BEANS.—Select young and tender beans. Wash thoroughly. Remove stems and strings. Slice or cut in 1in. lengths. Pre-cook 4 to 5 minutes in boiling water to cover. Pack in clean, hot jars. Add ½ teaspoon salt to each 1 lb. jar. Cover with boiling liquid in which beans were pre-cooked. Adjust lids. Process in Cooker according to Time Table.

BEETROOT.—Select young, tender, sweet beetroot. Trim off tops all but about 1in. of them. Leave these tap roots to prevent bleeding out. Wash thoroughly. Pre-cook in hot water for about 15 minutes, or until skins slip off easily. Remove skins, roots and stems. Small beetroot may be left whole, while larger ones are best sliced. Pack in hot, clean jars. Add 1 teaspoon salt and ½ teaspoon vinegar to each 1 lb. jar. Cover beetroot with boiling liquid. Adjust lids. Process according to Time Table.

CARROTS.—Select young and tender carrots. Sort according to size. Wash thoroughly and scrape. Carrots may be left whole or diced. Pre-cook in water to cover for 3-5 minutes, depending on size of carrots. Pack in hot, clean jars. Add ½ teaspoon salt to each 1 lb. jar. Cover with boiling liquid in which carrots have been pre-cooked. Adjust lids. Process according to Time Table.

GREENS.—Select young and tender greens. Sort thoroughly, discarding any wilted leaves, tougher stalks and roots. Wash well in several waters. Pre-cook in a small amount of boiling water for 2 to 3 minutes. Pack loosely in hot, clean jars. Add ½ teaspoon salt to each 1 lb. jar. Adjust lids. Process in Cooker according to Time Table.

MUSHROOMS.—Wash and remove stalks and skin if necessary. Cut larger mushrooms in smaller pieces. Drop in water containing 1 teaspoon of vinegar to each quart of water until ready for use to prevent darkening. Pre-cook mushrooms in boiling water for 3 minutes. Pack in clean, hot jars. Cover with boiling water in which they have been cooked. Add ½ teaspoon salt to each 1 lb. jar. Adjust lids. Process in Cooker according to Time Table.

PARSNIPS.—Wash parsnips thoroughly. Remove skins. Small, young parsnips may be bottled whole. If larger, they should be sliced or diced. Pre-cook in boiling water for 5 minutes. Pack in hot, clean jars. Add ½ teaspoon salt to each 1 lb. jar. Cover with boiling water in which they have been cooked. Adjust lids. Process in Cooker according to Time Table.

PEAS.—Select young, tender, freshly-picked peas. Wash pods and shell. Wash peas. Pre-cook in boiling water for 5 minutes. Pack loosely in hot, clean jars. Add ½ teaspoon salt to each 1 lb. jar. Cover with boiling, fresh water. Adjust lids. Process in Cooker according to Time Table.

TOMATOES.—Select fresh, ripe, unblemished tomatoes, of medium size. Dip into boiling water for 1 minute to loosen skins. Plunge in cold water. Remove skins. Put in a pan and cover with water. Bring just to boiling point. Pack in hot, clean jars. Add ½ teaspoon salt to each 1 lb. jar. No extra water is required, as tomatoes yield sufficient liquid. Process in Cooker according to Time Table.

| Vegetable | Pressure | Times for Glass Jars (1 lb. & 2 lb.) in Minutes |
|---|---|---|
| Asparagus | 10 | 25 |
| Beans, French and Runner | 10 | 20 |
| Beetroot | 10 | 25 |
| Carrots | 10 | 20 |
| Greens | 10 | 45 |
| Mushrooms | 10 | 35 |
| Parsnips | 10 | 35 |
| Peas (1 lb. jars only) | 10 | 40 |
| Tomatoes | 5 | 10 |